SNOW

BILL McAULIFFE

SCIENCE OF THE SKIES

Published by Creative Education
P.O. Box 227, Mankato, Minnesota 56002
Creative Education is an imprint of The Creative Company
www.thecreativecompany.us

Design and production by Liddy Walseth
Art direction by Rita Marshall
Printed by Corporate Graphics in the United States of America

Photographs by Alamy (Arco Images GmbH, StockShot), Corbis (Bettmann, Frans Lanting, Bill Stevenson/Aurora Photos), Dreamstime (James Steidl), Getty Images (Agence Zoom, Arctic-Images, Per Breiehagen, Rebecca Emery, Mitchell Funk, Dave Greenwood, David W. Hamilton, William Henry Jackson/George Eastman House, Johner, Froemel Kapitza, George Marks, David McNew, Michael Melford, Joe Raedle, Norbert Rosing, Sami Sarkis), iStockphoto (Todd Bates, James Boulette, Matthew Dula, Evelin Elmest, Alexander Hafemann, Julia Razumovitch, Ashok Rodrigues, Jerome Skiba, Andrzej Stajer)

Library of Congress Cataloging-in-Publication Data
McAuliffe, Bill.
Snow / by Bill McAuliffe.
p. cm. — (Science of the skies)
Summary: An exploration of snow, including how these icy flakes of precipitation develop, the ways in which snow affects everyday life, and how large snowstorms have impacted human history.
Includes bibliographical references and index.
ISBN 978-1-58341-929-8
1. Snow—Juvenile literature. I. Title.

QC926.37.M42 2010
551.57'84—dc22 2009023527

CPSIA: 120109 PO1095

First Edition
2 4 6 8 9 7 5 3 1

CREATIVE C EDUCATION

SNOW

BILL McAULIFFE

SCIENCE OF THE SKIES

FLODELLA FREEBY WAS ONE OF THOUSANDS OF PEOPLE ON THE MID-WESTERN PRAIRIE SURPRISED BY THE BLIZZARD OF NOVEMBER 11, 1940. MANY WERE DUCK HUNTERS, DRESSED IN LIGHT JACKETS ON WHAT HAD BEEN A WARM DAY. FREEBY'S CIRCUMSTANCES WERE DIFFERENT: SHE WAS STUCK IN A MINNESOTA FARMHOUSE, READY TO DELIVER A BABY. "THE CURTAIN OF WINTER CAME DOWN LIKE A VENETIAN BLIND WITH A BRO-KEN PULL-CORD," FREEBY RECALLED YEARS LATER. HER FATHER AND HUS-BAND TRIED TO DRIVE HER TO A HOSPITAL, BUT THEIR CAR GOT STUCK. THE THREE HIKED THROUGH HEAD-DEEP **DRIFTS** TO A FARMHOUSE, WHERE FREEBY DELIVERED HER BABY. FREEBY'S ARMISTICE DAY BLIZZARD STORY SHOWS MANY OF THE CONTRADICTORY QUALITIES OF SNOW. IT'S BEAUTI-FUL, AND IT'S THREATENING. IT'S ISOLATING, AND IT BRINGS PEOPLE TO-GETHER. IT'S ICE, BUT IT'S PILLOW-LIKE. THE STORM CLAIMED 154 LIVES ACROSS THE MIDWEST, BUT IT BROUGHT OUT THE RESOURCEFULNESS AND DETERMINATION OF MANY OTHERS.

In the cold parts of the world, the first snowfall of the year is usually no surprise. The temperature has been falling for weeks, the skies have been getting grayer, and shovels have been prominently displayed in hardware stores. But snow begins as something we don't associate with the freezing landscape. It begins with the warmth of the sun.

As the sun warms the earth, moisture is lifted into the air and **evaporates**. Because warm air rises, it lifts the water vapor higher and higher into the air, to a point where it gets chilled and **condenses** into tiny visible droplets, making a cloud. If the cloud gets lifted high enough into colder air, the droplets can freeze. Sometimes they form into icy balls of hail or **graupel**. But when conditions are right, they turn into the delicate sequins we know as snow.

Depending on how cold it is where the droplets freeze, they form ice crystals of different designs. At just below freezing (32 °F or 0 °C), they form six-sided plates. At 27 to 23 °F (–3 to –5 °C), they become needles. Getting colder, from 23 to 18 °F (–5 to –8 °C) they form hollow columns. When the air temperature is between 18 and 10 °F (–8 and -12 °C), they mysteriously prefer to become plates again. But from 10 °F down to 3 °F (–12 to –16 °C), they shift into star-shaped **dendrites**, while from 3 to –8 °F (–16 to –22 °C) they

return again to the familiar plate shape. Below those frigid temperatures, they once again adopt the hollow column shape. As the crystals fall into warmer air, they change into the shapes specific to that temperature range, and the same goes for when air currents carry them back aloft.

No matter what design the crystals are, though, they are all six-sided. That's also why the snowflakes that are built from them are six-sided or six-pointed. But a lot happens in the change from water to crystals to snowflakes. Remember, it all started with droplets of water. **Molecules** of water are attracted to one another, and when they combine, they form a six-sided shape, because of how water molecules are shaped. When they freeze, they do the same. And when they've formed crystals and are being tossed about in a cloud, they attract more and more water molecules,

YOU WANT IT?
YOU MAKE IT

Farmers have long sought a way to make rain to help their crops. But when ski resort operators or filmmakers need snow, they just fire up their machines. Snow-making machines create a spray of water droplets which, blown into air that's 32 °F (0 °C) or colder, turn into ice crystals. The crystals don't develop into six-sided snowflakes—just tiny bits of ice. But computers monitoring weather conditions around a ski resort can tell the machines to make varying kinds of "snow" and how much. The bad news? The process uses tremendous amounts of water and electricity.

which freeze onto them, continuing the six-sided construction. This explains why snowflakes, which are actually collections of anywhere from 2 to 200 ice crystals stuck to one another, have 6 sides.

Everybody knows that no two snowflakes are alike. But how do we know it for certain? It's more accurate to say that nobody has ever *seen* two identical snow-flakes and probably never will. To begin with, snow-flakes are far more similar to one another than they are different. The countless billions of snowflakes in any particular snowfall resemble one another as much as family members, because they have all formed and fallen at certain temperatures. Yet they might be quite different from those in a different snowfall in the same exact place, perhaps only minutes apart, because they formed and fell in different conditions. That's partly why snowfall depths are difficult to predict. Even though snowflakes are virtually all made on the same pattern and in the same way, the wild variety of forces

By the time the average snowflake reaches the ground, it may be composed of as many as 50,000 individual water droplets that have frozen into a 6-sided form.

Even though most snowflake photos taken through microscopes show flakes that are almost perfectly symmetrical, the typical snowflake is visibly irregular.

that they endure—updrafts, gravity, melting, refreezing, taking on more water and ice, collisions with each other and with dust and pollutants in the atmosphere—reshape each of them as they travel between the clouds and Earth. As a result, it's very likely that each one is unique.

Even after they come to rest on the ground, snowflakes continue to change shape. They might break as they fall or collapse under the weight of others falling on top of them. They might melt from warmth left in the ground, from the sun's radiation penetrating the snow and warming the darker ground beneath, or from warming air temperatures. They might compact or erode into a heavy, icy powder. Ultimately, by the time winter is ending, they might not resemble snow as much as a mass of small granules of ice, much like what you find in the icy treat somewhat inaccurately called a snow cone.

Still, whether it's new, dry, and full of pointy snowflakes or old, wet, and turning into rounded globs of ice, snow always appears white. Sometimes it will take on other hues, such as red, but that's often due to impurities in the air or in the water from which it started, or from tainting by algae or other substances. Pure snow is white, because, in fact, it's clear.

Snow is sometimes said to turn landscapes into "winter wonderlands," as the uniform whiteness of snow on ground and frost on trees can dramatically alter a place.

Snow in any condition is simply many, many crystals of ice, which are clear. When light passes through ice or water, it gets broken up into all colors, in the same way a rainbow is formed by the sun shining through raindrops. In a pile of snow, these beams of color simply get bounced around—mostly through air—without being absorbed and are sent back to the viewing eye, which perceives them altogether as white.

There are some delightful exceptions to snow's color, though. When new snow covers the ground on a bright, sunny day, it can sparkle with flashes of distinct random colors—red, blue, yellow, and combinations of them, such as orange and green. This happens when beams of light pass through ice crystals on the very top layer of snow, are broken up into colors, and reflect back to us at different angles, much the way light interacts with diamonds. Together they are white, but under the right light and snow conditions, and seen from random angles, they give us a sparkling and unexpected array of colors.

Yet glaciers and even holes poked in deep, fresh snow have a vivid blue color. This is because blue light is able to penetrate deeper than other colors into snow or ice that has less air in it. Glaciers are in fact snow that has been compacted for thousands of years by repeated snowfalls, so the bluer the glacier, the less air it contains and the older it is. People who work and play on ice know that blue ice is always stronger than white ice, which tends to be young and airy.

No matter if they are in Norway (below) or Antarctica (right), all glaciers become bluer in color toward their bottoms, where old snow and ice are densely compacted.

A MAN NAMED "SNOWFLAKE"

Winter is often a time for farmers in snowy Vermont to take it easy. But that's when Wilson Alwyn Bentley did his most important work. Beginning in 1885, Bentley photographed individual snowflakes for more than 45 years, producing more than 6,000 microscopic photos that revealed the delicately icy structure of snow. Bentley, who also played a variety of musical instruments and composed music for a community band in Jericho, Vermont, soon was nicknamed "Snowflake." In 1920, he was elected Fellow of the American Meteorological Society. And yes, among all his photos, no two snowflakes were alike.

HOW DEEP IS
"KNEE-DEEP"?

Measuring snow is one of the trickiest and least precise weather observation activities. It's also one of the most obvious and least technical. Basically, measuring snow requires a flat surface in an open but protected area to catch snow, as well as a ruler to measure it. A pair of boots and gloves helps, too, since the measurer has to walk through snow and handle it.

A day's snowfall, or snow in a single storm or over the course of several hours, is measured on a flat surface that can be wiped off. In most cases, that's a board (preferably white, since anything dark would warm up and possibly melt the snow). A board about 16 to 24 inches (40–61 cm) square is usually placed on the ground and marked with a small flag or stick so it can be found when the snow is deep.

People who measure snow as a hobby sometimes have difficulties doing so in backyards, since kids, pets, and birds can step on the snow board and mess up a new snowfall. And in places that don't receive heavy snowfall, the wind can often blow snow around and make measuring difficult.

Aside from such complications, taking a snow measurement is simple. Using a ruler that breaks inches into tenths (or, in Canada and much of the rest of the world, a ruler marked in centimeters), the measurer will check the depth of the new snow on the board, then wipe it off. That represents the day's or storm's snowfall. If there are varying depths on the board, usually from wind, an average of several depths is considered accurate. In a heavy storm, or when the snow is particularly wet and packing down, the observer might take a measurement every hour and add up the readings for a single day or a single storm within a day. Snow that melts as it falls is recorded as a **trace**. Volunteers and officials with the National Weather Service record new snow only once every six hours at the most.

Although precise snowfall measurements are important to weather professionals, the average person is more likely to evaluate snowfall amounts by how difficult they make travel.

Snow depth is a little different. That's the snow that has remained on the ground, usually for the season, enduring melting, refreezing, packing, evaporation, wind effects, and other changes. It's nearly always less than the sum of all the individual snowfalls in a winter. For example, the snowfall for a winter month in Milwaukee, Wisconsin, might measure 14 inches (35 cm), but the deepest snow cover on any day within that month might have been 8 inches (20 cm), or even less.

Observers measure snow depth once a day in an open area where, ideally, there's not much drifting or clearing from the wind, or other disturbances. They'll take measurements in several spots, ideally atop a hard surface, since grass is soft and uneven and doesn't provide accurate depths. Observers will average those readings and round them to the nearest inch or centimeter.

Wide expanses such as New York City's Central Park may present snow undisturbed by human activity, but blowing winds in such spaces can hinder snow measurements.

AN EPIC, SNOWY TRAGEDY

When the Donner Party, a group of pioneers traveling from Illinois to California in 1846, reached the Sierra Nevada mountains in early September, snow was already on the trail. In early November, they were trapped by snow 12 feet (3.6 m) deep. Many starved, and some of the others resorted to cannibalism. By the time the last of the survivors were rescued in April, 41 of the original 87 travelers had perished. Snow wasn't precisely measured in those days, but between 1880 and 2005, the trail that came to be known as Donner Pass had 10 winters with 50 feet (15 m) or more of snow.

Of course, the wind makes this measurement troublesome, too, and often pushes it into the realm of guesswork. Observers aren't supposed to include the depths of drifts in their measurements. But where there's a combination of bare ground and drifts in the measuring area, the National Weather Service encourages observers to use "good judgment" in coming up with an average. One National Oceanic and Atmospheric Administration (NOAA) instruction sheet recommends that anyone measuring snow depth after winds have blown new snow around "make a good guess on how much new snow fell."

Before weather measurements started to become standardized in the late 1800s in the United States, snow depths were described by comparisons most people were familiar with from their everyday lives. Snow was "knee-high" or "up to the windowsills" or "not enough to hide a mouse." Today's measurements of snowfalls and seasonal snow depth, averaged much more precisely over the span of many years, are often quoted with pride to suggest a city or region's strong wintry character.

The snowiest national capital in the world is not in Russia, Nepal, or Switzerland, as one might guess. The honor instead goes to Ottawa, Ontario, where 93 inches (236 cm) of snow fall in an average winter.

Due to the high mountain elevations (up to 15,200 feet, or 4,630 m) of the Alps, Switzerland has long been regarded as one of the world's great lands of snow.

(Ottawa is still only the 34th snowiest city in Canada, however. Gander, Newfoundland, gets 169 inches [443 cm] of snow in a typical winter.)

In the U.S., the snowiest city is Valdez, Alaska, a seaside town of 4,000 people amid glaciers and mountains where 325 inches (825 cm) are expected every year. Because the climate there is moist and mild, the snow in Valdez tends to be wet and heavy. To deal with it, many homes have steep roofs made of metal that allow the white stuff to slide off. However, it then often covers first-floor windows, and residents are encouraged to plow the snow away from the sides of their houses to prevent melting snow from leaking in. After Valdez was heavily damaged by an earthquake in 1964, it was rebuilt four miles (6.4 km) away. The new city was laid out with extra-wide streets with vacant strips down the middles so snow plowed off the streets could be piled there.

The city of Marquette, Michigan, on the south shore of Lake Superior, gets about 141 inches (358 cm) of snow each winter, making it the snowiest city in the **continental U.S.** But among much larger cities, several in upstate New York are famous for deep snow. Syracuse receives about 115 inches (292 cm) of snow each year, and its airport has boasted of using the world's largest snowplow—32 feet (9.8 m) wide—to clear snow from its runways. Nearby Buffalo sees about 94 inches (239 cm), and Rochester gets 92 inches (234 cm). The reason? These cities are located along the eastern shores of two of the Great Lakes. **Prevailing winds** from the west pick up moisture from the lakes (which often don't freeze over entirely), lift it into the air, where it turns into snow, and drop it in great quantities shortly after they encounter land. These cities often receive tremendous dumps of snow all at once. In 2001, Buffalo received 82 inches (208 cm) of snow in only 5 days over the Christmas holiday, including 27 inches (69 cm) on the fifth day. When the long storm was over, the National Weather Service measured 45 inches (114 cm) on the ground—nearly 4 feet (1.2 m). That was enough to get people bragging. "Buffalo is king at last!" one local publication blared.

The potential for massive snowfall is greatest where large bodies of water offer up moisture, such as at Lake Michigan ports (top) and Valdez, Alaska (bottom).

A KILLER ON THE SLOPES

Avalanches kill more than 150 people around the world each year. In recent years in the U.S. and Canada, those killed have most commonly been snowmobilers. A large avalanche can carry the same amount of snow as 20 football fields covered 10 feet (3 m) deep, flattening trees as it moves. Many victims of avalanches suffocate in the packed snow. For a person caught in sliding snow, one survival strategy is to use a swimming motion to try to stay near the top of the snow. Fresh snow, warming temperatures, steep slopes, and deep snows on the downwind sides of mountains increase the risk of avalanches.

ADVARSEL!

HER FORLATER DU DET MERKEDE
OG SIKREDE SKIOMRÅDET.
ALL SKIKJØRING PÅ EGET ANSVAR!

WARNING!

OFF-PISTE SECTOR
NEITHER SIGNED - NOR PATROLLED
THIS SKIING IS DONE ENTIRELY ON
YOUR OWN RISK AND RESPONSIBILITY

TENK
SKREDFARE
AVALANCH
ALERT
ACHTUNG
LAWINENGEFAHR

Snow makes a difference. Unlike rain or just about anything else that falls from the sky, snow remakes the identity of a place, changing it overnight into a white fantasy land—or a land of nightmarish inconvenience. It energizes entire recreational industries, from skiing and snowmobiling to winter carnivals, and adds appeal to their opposites—the midwinter Mexican vacation or the Arizona retirement. It prompts people to change their footwear and animals to change their colors. It means challenges for travel, whether it's walking or flying. It conjures up cozy and cheerful images of snowmen and hot chocolate, **igloos** and fireplaces, mittens and snow days.

Many people in the world have never seen snow or live in places where it never snows. Although most of the world's snow and ice cover occurs in the Northern Hemisphere, snow covers only about one-fourth of the hemisphere's landmasses in January. A satellite view of Earth from above the North Pole in winter shows how little of the planet is covered with snow.

But snow is still a powerful image and idea around the world. That may be because snowy countries, such as Russia, Germany, the U.S., and Japan, have dominated the world's **commerce**, warfare, and culture in recent centuries. For example, Christmas is commonly associated with snow, even though the birth of Christ took place in the Middle East, where snow is extremely rare. Snowy Christmas imagery likely grew from the celebration of the holiday, through stories and music, in Germany, England, and the U.S.

So you might consider yourself lucky if you live where it snows. For several months of the year, you can snowboard or ski, build a fort, or have a snowball fight. Snow can be a good excuse to have a lot of fun. But it also poses challenges, primarily to movement. Humans have been figuring out new ways to move on or through snow for thousands of years. About 6,000 years ago, people living in what is now Sweden strapped pieces of wood to their feet to slide across deep snow while traveling and hunting. Those were the first known skis. At about the same time, people in central Asia started using webbed platforms for walking through deep snow, and it's believed the invention was brought to North America by descendants of those early snowshoers.

In locales where winter represents a dramatic change of season, such as in New York, many people welcome the arrival of snow for its beauty and holiday ambiance.

In the 1700s, Scandinavians developed skiing as a sport, refining ways to turn on skis and even promoting ski jumping. Skiing became part of the Olympics in 1924 and soon afterward began to gain wide popularity in North America. In the late 1940s, after the end of World War II, skiing had such potential to attract sporting types and winter tourists that inventors in New England got together and designed machines to make snow for those times when the sky wouldn't. Skiing has also been used in warfare since the early 1800s and was employed to great advantage by both the Finns and Russians in World War II. Even in 2009, U.S. Army soldiers serving in the mountains of Afghanistan were trained in skiing and snowshoeing.

People have long had horses, sleighs, sleds, toboggans, and other means to travel across snow. But it was inevitable that they would want engines to push them through snowy country. The Russians developed what might be regarded as the first snowmobile, a sort of small tank on skis that was driven by a propeller, in about 1910. Soon, in the U.S. and Canada, inventors were experimenting with skis and tracks attached to a Model T **chassis**, and a New Hampshire Ford dealer

and tinkerer named Virgil White built what he called a snowmobile in 1913. In Quebec, Joseph-Armand Bombardier, whose name became linked with the widespread popularity of snowmobiles, built his first one in 1922 at the age of 15. Forty-six years later, his nephew Jean-Luc was part of the first expedition to reach the North Pole by snowmobile.

Snow itself also has significant value to people. About 70 percent of the water supply in the western U.S. ultimately comes from melting snows in the Rocky Mountains and other nearby ranges. That snow also

Unlike other forms of precipitation, snow presents opportunities for many forms of recreation, from snowmobiling to skiing (opposite) to snowshoeing (below).

MAKING IT GO AWAY

You can shovel it. You can plow it. You can haul it away in trucks. Those are the most common ways of getting snow off sidewalks, roads, and airport runways. But there are some other ways of clearing snow. In Ottawa, Ontario, crews sometimes push plowed snow back onto roads once the roads are warm enough to melt it. At Minnesota's Minneapolis–St. Paul International Airport, heated pools of water can melt 120 tons (109 t) of snow per hour. The melters reduce the need to spread salt or other chemicals on pavement to keep snow from accumulating, which is better for the surrounding environment.

drains into rivers that flow eastward and feed the Mississippi and Missouri rivers, which provide drinking water for millions of residents in towns and cities across the Great Plains and **irrigate** thousands of acres of crops. On the other side of the globe, melting snow in the Himalayas supplies rivers that are water sources for more than half a billion people in central Asia.

Even when it's still in its frozen form, snow can be a valuable resource. In the far north, native people have long used snow packed by the wind to build igloos for shelter, cutting blocks of snow and arranging them into a thick-walled, frozen tent. One of the reasons igloos provide excellent shelter is that snow, while cold, is actually a very effective insulator. The many surfaces of the flakes in snow can trap and hold warm air in place. This is why animals and even hardy winter campers will find it more comfortable to sleep in deep snow than in the open. Once snow melts into water, however, it loses its insulating capacity, because water conducts heat away from its source. So while an igloo—or even a mouse's tunnel under the snow— might be much warmer inside than the surrounding winter landscape, it's most effective only at or below 32 °F (0 °C). At warmer temperatures, the igloo begins to melt, losing its heat-trapping qualities and maybe even collapsing.

WAY MORE THAN "WHITE STUFF"

It's widely believed that the Inuit have hundreds of words for snow. But that's not quite true. According to Lawrence Kaplan, director of the Alaskan Native Language Center in Fairbanks, Alaska, native Arctic peoples have many words for different types of snow or snow conditions, but many are words for other things as well. For example, *mapsa* refers to a type of overhanging snow but is also the word for the human spleen, which hangs in the same way over the stomach. Scientists, whose microscopes have identified many more snow shapes and structures than were previously known, have more than 100 different names for snow.

While snow can trap heat, it also reflects the sun's radiation. It is this property, known as **albedo**, that has caused climate scientists to monitor Earth's snow cover very closely. Many are worried that if global warming were to lead to less snow on the ground, areas that were previously white and able to reflect the sun's radiation back into space would instead absorb radiation and speed up the warming process.

Scientists who worry about the threat of global warming pay attention to snow cover on Nepal's Himalaya Mountains and other landscapes where snow is a constant.

HUMBLING, DISRUPTIVE AND FATAL

The early months of 1888 brought two of the most memorable blizzards in U.S. history. One crippled the great cities of the eastern seaboard, while the other brought sudden and ghastly tragedy to the farms and small towns of the northern Great Plains.

The morning of January 12 was unseasonably warm across the Dakota Territory (what is now North and South Dakota). Many parents sent their children to school lightly dressed, while farmers headed out into the fields dressed more for spring than deep winter. But a cold front tore across the region with such speed and force that many people were fatally trapped. The temperature dropped 18 °F (10 °C) in three minutes, and the air filled with snow. Across the land, teachers in one-room schools had to decide whether to send their students home or to keep them at the school-house. Many of those struggling to get home froze to death in windchills that reached 40 °F below zero (–40 °C); other students died with their teachers, often while trying to find other shelter. Five boys in one family died. Some people suffocated, unable to breathe in the snow-filled air.

Between 250 and 500 people perished in the storm—so many of them were children that the storm has become known as "The Children's Blizzard." Author David Laskin, in his 2004 book about the tragedy, *The Children's Blizzard*, suggests that the storm changed the way many of the immigrant settlers in the region came to view the land, leading them to fear a place they had previously seen as full of promise.

Two months later, on March 11, a storm buried New York City under more than 3 feet (0.9 m) of snow, driven by winds of 70 miles (113 km) per hour. A 52-foot (15.8 m) drift was documented in the Gravesend neighborhood. Thirty people died in the city after trying to get to work, only to find their offices and factories shut down for lack of electricity. Food became scarce, and some people were unable to dig out of their homes for weeks. Ultimately, about 400 people died across New England, including 200 in New York City.

Despite modern forecasting technology, snow always has the potential to cause serious problems for people, whether they live in rural isolation or amid big-city bustle.

The proud city—the capital of U.S. commerce—was humbled by impassable streets, snow-covered train tracks, and a communication system that collapsed as wires and telegraph poles fell under the weight of snow. Even the Brooklyn Bridge, an engineering triumph completed only five years before, was closed. But the disaster eventually transformed New York and other cities on the East Coast for the better. New York quickly moved to put its telephone and telegraph wires underground, where snow couldn't affect them. Up the seaboard in Boston, Massachusetts, the blizzard led to the development of the first subway system in the country.

In his 1997 book *Snow in America*, author Bernard Mergen notes that it was the railroads that pioneered snow removal and snow-protection structures. By the 1870s, railroad companies were building roofs over their tracks through mountainous, snowy passes to keep avalanches from closing the routes. They were also lining the routes with **snow fences**, an innovation adopted from northern Europe, to reduce the effects of drifting. Soon they were using gigantic plow blades, pushed by locomotives, to clear snow from tracks. By the 1890s, railroad companies had developed rotary plowing machines, which worked much like today's **snowblowers**. These machines were mounted to the

fronts of train engines and threw the snow off the tracks to one side or the other.

Even so, passengers on long-distance trips through snowy country in those days were often pressed into service clearing tracks the old-fashioned way: with shovels. And as if to further mock people's attempts at industrial-scale snow-proofing, an avalanche along the Great Northern Railway in the mountains of eastern Washington in February 1910 claimed the lives of 96 people. Most of the victims had been passengers on two trains that were stalled for six days by snow. Twenty-two survived, but the number of deaths is still the highest of any avalanche incident in U.S. history.

Despite advances in snow removal and aggressive street-clearing policies in cities, snow and crowded urban environments remained a troubled combination into the 21st century. In January 1922, a blizzard dropped more than 24 inches (61 cm) of wet snow on Washington, D.C., causing the roof of the Knickerbocker Theater to collapse, which killed more than 100 people. A snow-and-rain storm that ran up the Appalachian Mountains in November 1950 dumped 30 inches (76 cm) of snow on Pittsburgh, Pennsylvania, and 24 inches (61 m) on Cleveland, Ohio. In all, 160 people died.

Although rotary plowing machines (opposite) improved train travel in the late 1800s, railways and snowy mountains are still a precarious pairing.

Great blizzards and snowstorms in more recent years have not killed as many people. But as the population has increased and more vehicles have been traveling the roads, even minor snowfalls now stall city traffic. Similarly, because air traffic has also increased, a blizzard or large snowfall in one major U.S. or Canadian city can leave people stranded and sleeping in airports across the continent, sometimes for days. When power lines collapse under the weight of snow, millions of people across vast regions can lose light, heat, access to food, and supplies for long periods. Snow also costs taxpayers money. In New York City, the cost of snow removal is estimated to be $1 million per inch (2.5 cm).

Great snowfalls can also affect jobs—particularly those of city leaders. In January 1979, a blizzard that ultimately killed 99 people effectively ruined the career of Chicago, Illinois, mayor Michael Bilandic. A 20-inch (50 cm) snowfall, on top of 7 inches (18 cm) already on the ground, put a stranglehold on the city. Roofs collapsed, garbage trucks couldn't pick up trash, and many of the city's famous elevated trains couldn't run, as snow either packed the tracks or blew into the trains' electric motors, disabling them. O'Hare International Airport, then the world's busiest, had only half its runways open six days after the storm. The problems reminded residents all too much of a similar blizzard and its complications

MEASURING WATER WITHOUT GETTING WET

One of the things that scientists, flood forecasters, and emergency planners want to know about snow is how much water it contains. They find this out from measurements taken by NOAA planes. Flying 500 feet (152 m) above snow, the planes measure radiation, or heat energy, emitted by the soil. Because water blocks or reduces a certain type of radiation, researchers can determine how much water is in the snow. It's commonly believed that 1 inch (2.5 cm) of precipitation makes 10 inches (25 cm) of snow, but that is typically true for only wet snow. Across much of the northern U.S. and Canada, the average ratio is 1:15.

BLIZZARD BULLETIN

The word "blizzard" once referred to a group of rapid punches in a boxing match. (Of course, that's also known by another snowy term: a "flurry.") It was the Estherville, Iowa , newspaper Northern Vindicator *that first used the word to describe a snowstorm on April 23, 1870. Today, "blizzard" has a specific meaning: wintry conditions including sustained winds or gusts of at least 35 miles (56 km) per hour, and falling or blowing snow that reduces visibility to one-quarter mile (400 m). That's in the U.S.; in Canada, it's 25 miles (40 km) per hour winds and visibility of .62 mile (1 km).*

only 12 years before. Six weeks later, Bilandic lost an election against an opponent he had earlier been expected to trounce.

Historians say Mayor Bilandic really lost to the snow. And that's not much of an exaggeration. Snow has proven itself time and again to be a powerful foe, as well as a useful friend. And often it's the snow that decides which it will be.

A paradox on many levels, snow is capable of simultaneously beautifying the environment (opposite) and causing urban nightmares (as in Chicago in 1979, below).

GLOSSARY

ALBEDO, n. — *light from the sun that is reflected off snow or a similar surface*

AVALANCHES, n. — *falls or slides of large masses of snow, rock, or other material down a mountainside*

CANNIBALISM, n. — *the act of humans eating the flesh of other humans*

CHASSIS, n. — *the steel frame that holds the body and motor of a vehicle*

COMMERCE, n. — *the buying and selling of goods; business or trade*

CONDENSES, v. — *forms a liquid from a vapor*

CONTINENTAL U.S., n. — *the 48 American states that are connected to one another; the other two are Alaska and Hawaii*

DENDRITES, n. — *branchlike growths*

DRIFTS, n. — *peaks, ridges, or solid waves of snow created by wind*

EVAPORATES, v. — *turns from a liquid into a vapor*

GRAUPEL, n. — *a collection of tiny, white, ball-like masses of ice that each form around a snowflake and fall to the ground resembling bits of Styrofoam*

IGLOOS, n. — *domed shelters made from blocks of snow*

IRRIGATE, v. — *to draw water from underground or from streams and rivers and spread it over farm fields*

MOLECULES, n. — *groupings of two or more atoms; they make up the smallest and most fundamental unit of a substance*

PREVAILING WINDS, n. — *winds that blow most often from one particular direction*

SNOWBLOWERS, n. — *machines that pick up snow and blow or throw it aside; they are most commonly used to clear household driveways and sidewalks*

SNOW FENCES, n. — *barriers, usually of wood or trees, built or planted in windy areas to control or lessen the drifting of snow*

TRACE, n. — *a measurement of snow or rain that's less than the minimum that can be measured; for snow, that would be less than 0.1 inch (2.5 mm), and for rain, less than .01 inch (.25 mm)*

Farndon, John. *Extreme Weather*. London: Dorling Kindersley, 2007.

Jenkins, McKay. *The White Death: Tragedy and Heroism in an Avalanche Zone*. New York: Random House, 2000.

Laskin, David. *The Children's Blizzard*. New York: HarperCollins, 2004.

Mergen, Bernard. *Snow in America*. Washington, D.C.: Smithsonian Institution Press, 1999.

Physical Science. "A Closer Look: Why do Snowflakes Have Six Sides?" Annenberg Media. http://www.learner.org/courses/essential/physicalsci/session6/closer1.html.

Science Fact Finder. "How Does Snow Form?" Enotes.com. http://www.enotes.com/science-fact-finder/weather-climate/how-does-snow-form.

SpaceRef.com. "NASA Scientists in Dogged Pursuit of Amount of Snow on Earth Embark on Arctic Trek." Goddard Space Flight Center. http://www.spaceref.com/news/viewpr.html?pid=19301.

INDEX